British Electric Tramways

A Belfast scene in 1953 illustrating two types of the original fleet of 441 electric tramcars owned by Belfast Corporation. The leading car No 357 was built in 1930 and it is preserved in Belfast Transport Museum; the car following is of a very luxurious modern design built after 1935.

British Electric Tramways

E. Jackson-Stevens

David & Charles : Newton Abbot

ISBN   0 7153 5105 2

Set in 10 on 12-point Plantin
and printed in Great Britain
by W J Holman Limited Dawlish
for David & Charles (Publishers) Limited
South Devon House Newton Abbot Devon

Contents

Going home from business, 1933: a London tramcar in the evening rush-hour at Bloomsbury. The trams, with their cheap tickets, provided bargain travel for generations of Londoners.

Introduction

Soon a whole generation will have grown up which never knew anything about the characteristics of the efficient electric tramcars which graced the streets of Great Britain in the closing years of the last century and the first half of this one. It seems a far cry, in these days of traffic-congestion where the ubiquitous motor car succeeds in defeating its own primary purpose, to realise that these same cities and towns were once served by a clean, fumeless, swiftly accelerating and remarkably cheap form of transport, exceptionally reliable and competent.

Probably one of the most striking aspects of the history of the British tramcar since its deplorable demise, is the insatiable thirst of the younger generation for more knowledge of its fascination, the intricacies of its operation, the legal considerations and the constructional and engineering problems encountered and overcome. Above all else, however, is the irresistible attraction of the tramcar itself with its distinguishing localised features differing in some degree in various areas. In an age where individuality is so subservient to an over-emphasis on standardisation in every walk of life, a methodical record of the development of electric tramcars of Britain, from the first trolley-line at Leeds on 8 January 1892 to the closures of the 1960s, would provide a vivid insight into an era also bedevilled by two world wars. Not only was this nation fortunate in being able to rely on a passenger transport system dependent upon home-produced fuel, but those cities and towns which had not discarded their tramway system before World War II benefitted by their foresight to a considerable degree. If the lesson was lost on Britain, it has certainly not been lost on some other nations for it is notable that very many cities in other countries have retained and extended their tramways and modernised them.

The commercial development and social interest of tramways is a vast subject, and the illustrations and theme in the following pages aim only to achieve a reasonable balance of the main attributes of British electric tramways. To do this I have made a personal selection of tramway pictures, choosing them in order to give a wide cross-section of Britain's electric tramways and to include a fairly high proportion of hitherto unpublished views. Many sources have been tapped—newspaper libraries, local authorities, manufacturers, transport operators, commercial street views and private collections—and I would like to record my thanks and my appreciation of their willing help.

E. JACKSON-STEVENS
Easter 1970

Glastonbury
Somerset

Electric Tramway Tracks and Trackwork

The rudimentary history of tramways precedes the history of railways as the first 'tramroad' was laid with tracks of wood, stone or iron for trams or waggons. Bad roads were the cause of the demand. Wood tracks were first tried but found unsatisfactory so iron bars were nailed on but these bent under the strain. In 1767 cast iron was tried with greater success, being laid on wooden railings. The load for one horse was about 8 bolls (17cwt) on the cart-tracks which passed for roadways but upon a tramway it was discovered that a horse could pull 19 bolls or 42cwt of coal. In the 1770s rails with flanges on the inside were commonly used but in 1789 William Jessop used cast iron rails, removing the flanges from the rails to the inner side of the wheels, a method which has become standard for tramways and railways since that time. The first street tramway was at Birkenhead in 1860, on track laid by George Francis Train who followed up his success by laying a track between Marble Arch and Notting Hill Gate, London. This track was soon taken up because the rails were laid on the road and not in it, thus causing obstructions to the free passage of other vehicles. Probably one of the greatest steps forward in the evolution of street tramways was the 'Crescent' rail patented in 1860. This was a rail flush with the roadway, at the same time providing a groove of such minor dimensions as to cause no inconvenience to other road users. The next progressive step was the passing of the Tramways Act of 1870, almost more reviled than any other statute. Although this Act simplified tramway projects, many clauses were damaging to tramways, the most notable being that tramway undertakings, in addition to paving the roadway between the track gauge, must also pave and maintain the road surface for 18in on either side of their tracks.

The illustration below shows a standard type of track construction, the concrete foundation (a), the bedding for the granite setts (b); with the granite paving (c). The paving was finished off by filling the interstices between the blocks with bitumen and pitch, completing with cement.

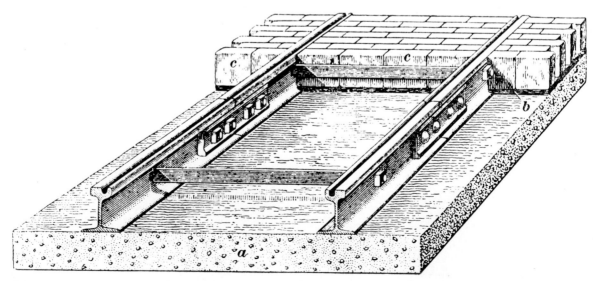

The clause in the Act designed to recompense local authorities in the days of horsedrawn tramcars was a burden never repealed in the days of electric traction, as our legislators steadfastly refused to believe that tramcars were electrically propelled and made no use of the paving, despite the fact that electric tramcars ran right under their noses, hard by the Houses of Parliament, for half a century. Granite setts were largely used in tramway paving because of their hard-wearing character. The illustration above shows a Glasgow permanent-way tram being loaded. Tramway undertakings had to maintain huge areas of roadway, for the benefit of other road-users including their competitors, the motor buses.

Tramway junctions and crossings, dependent on the street layout, were complicated and expensive, especially on the London conduit tramways. The renewal in 1927 of the five-way intersection at Aldgate was one of the largest engineering projects ever tackled.

A depot 'car-fan' of twenty-seven tracks constructed in manganese steel for Kirkstall Road Depot, Leeds. The intricacies of the labyrinth of pointwork and the rolled manganese guard-rails on the inner curves leading to the depot tracks illustrate a high degree of precision engineering. The manufacture of special tramway trackwork was a speciality of the Sheffield steel industry, and British-made tramway points and crossings were exported to most parts of the world.

Early Electric Tramway Systems

The electrification of the previous horse and steam tramways in Great Britain, and the extension of electric tramways was bedevilled by the ineptitude and incompetence of local authorities, which retarded early progress to a considerable degree. The British Electric Traction Company had extensive private enterprise plans frustrated by municipal obstruction, so while there were 2,540 miles of electric tramways in the USA in 1896, there were only 1,040 miles of tramway in Great Britain, still operated mainly by horse and steam tramcars. The passing of the Light Railway Act in 1896 went some way towards easing the heavy hand of bureaucracy, and between 1900 and 1907 the total mileage of electric tramways increased to 2,232. Even so, continued lack of vision by local authorities still retarded extensive development. Parochial-mindedness caused many systems to be laid to different gauges, thus preventing through running. The differing gauges, sometimes in adjoining towns, varied from 3ft 6in, 4ft, 4ft 7¾in, 4ft 8½in to the 5ft 3in of parts of Ireland. Tenacious petty jealousy and rivalry between neighbouring towns recoiled decisively to the detriment of electric tramways in later years. The illustration below is of the first electric tramcar running to Clapham on 15 May 1903. On the upper deck of a tramcar specially painted white for the occasion, the Prince of Wales (afterwards King George V) can be seen raising his hat in acknowledgement to the welcoming crowds.

Typical of the county, municipal and company disagreements which delayed progress of enterprising projects in the initial stages of the electric tramway era is that of Gloucester. In 1899 the City of Gloucester Tramways Company Limited wanted to electrify the existing horse tramways of that city. The corporation conditionally agreed not to oppose the application to the Light Railway Commissioners at their inquiry. Later the corporation broke off negotiations with the company in 1900, resulting in a year being lost. Suddenly, without consulting the interested parties, the county council applied for an order empowering them to construct and work a tramway from Brockworth to the city boundary. The city authorities considered this unreasonable as changing cars and waiting would have been involved. The horse tramways were finally purchased for £26,000 in September 1902, the system electrified and the first corporation electric tramcar eventually ran in May 1904. Five years of superfluous arguments for a small city system comprising a fleet of only thirty electric tramcars. The commissioners resolved the dispute between the city and county by authorising the county to construct the line between Wotton and Hucclecote, the corporation to bear the whole of the annual charge on the capital cost and pay an annual wayleave of £50 to the county council. It was the only county-owned tramway outside London. The illustration above is of an early Gloucester electric tramcar.

Even more acrimony attended the projects for the vast systems in the Midlands. The British Electric Traction Company Limited, after nearly obtaining a long lease to operate and electrify the tramways in the Birmingham area, next turned its attention to the surrounding Black Country and approached the many local authorities in 1900 with proposals to take over and electrify the various horse and steam tramway systems and operate them under one management. No uniform agreement could be negotiated and several different local companies were formed, with the BET as the parent company, to operate electric tramways in various areas of the Black Country. Additionally Walsall and Wolverhampton Corporations insisted on purchasing and operating their tramways themselves. West Bromwich, Dudley and Wednesbury also purchased their tramways but leased operation to th BET subsidiaries. Other smaller towns deferred purchase and were content to let their tramways be company operated.

The illustration above is of the first type of car used on the Dudley-Stourbridge system in 1900, typical of many of these tramcars in the Black Country at the inauguration of the various company-owned systems.

An outstanding feature of the new electric tramways was the cheap production of electric current on a large scale. Most undertakings, municipal and privately owned, built their own powerstations which, in addition to supplying their tramways with current at 550 volts dc also provided a lower voltage for residential consumers. The early power companies often had the appendage '. . . Electric Power & Traction Co Ltd' in their titles. In some cases the tramway bought the power instead of generating its own. Some tramway companies purchased their electric current from other privately owned power companies but there were also instances of municipally produced power being supplied to a privately owned tramway company, often with frequent wranglings and discords about the cost of the current. The classic example of this type of altercation was Taunton. When the corporation wanted to increase their tariff the tramway company would not agree. The power supply was abruptly discontinued on 28 May 1921 at night leaving, according to one version, a tramcar stranded at the far terminus which had to be towed back to the depot by a horse. This small system of tramcars never ran again. Below is an illustration of a tramcar in North Street, Taunton.

Opening of the widened Blackfriars Bridge, London, on 14 September 1909: the Lord Mayor driving the first London County Council tramcar across the bridge. With all the confident aplomb of a civic dignitary the eminent gentleman is quite oblivious of the fact that he is operating the controller with the wrong hand. Tramcar controllers are operated with the left hand.

Not all tramcars were of the double-deck type as some undertakings encountered the additional problem of low railway bridges spanning their routes and had to resort to single-deck tramcars. This illustration is an early Black Country 3ft 6in gauge tramcar. Below is the first electric tramcar to arrive at Kingswood from Old Market, Bristol, on 14 October 1895. The Lord Mayor of Bristol, the Chairman of Kingswood UDC, councillors and company officials are on board.

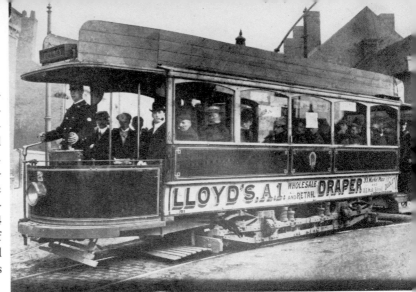

The Edwardian Scene

The years 1901 to 1910 were a period of expansion of electric tramways for, between the early experimental Leeds (January 1892), the South Staffordshire (January 1893), the Bristol (October 1895) and the end of the Edwardian period, 105 corporation and 74 company systems were inaugurated. It was a matter of civic pride for any pretentious British town to vie with its neighbour in an endeavour to prove its status by providing the most efficient and enterprising electric public transport system for its citizens, at extremely cheap fares, with a frequent and fast tramway service. In this era tramways were being extended to the suburbs as quickly as the housebuilding progressed. 'Trade follows the tramway' was a truism often heard and any highstreet not boasting an electric tramway was regarded as very Victorian. The photograph below of Christchurch, Hants is typical of a scene at the opening of a new tramway route during this period, with the new tramcars decorated specially for the event, tramwaymen in brand new uniforms and an interested populace posing to mark the occasion.

During the time of the great extensions the tramcar designers were only just beginning to give some thought to the comfort of passengers on the upper decks of the tramcars. The previous emphasis had been on an enclosed lower deck and an open top deck, the latter being ideal for the brief spring and summer days but not quite so comfortable in the rigours of a British winter. It soon became apparent that the upper decks would have to be enclosed too. In many cases they were although some of the smaller systems ran open-top tramcars throughout their life, while low bridge restrictions precluded top covers being fitted on other systems. Standard Edwardian British tramcars are seen (*above*) on the Lytham St Annes corporation tramway, and (*right*) on the Cambourne & Redruth Company tramway.

Old Market, Bristol (*above*) typifies an Edwardian electric tramway scene with its open-topped cars, centrally situated overhead standards surmounted by electric arc-lamps, then the last word in street lighting. The profusion of tramcars with a short headway between each indicates the ease with which townspeople could quickly traverse the city. The absence of traffic jams is also apparent.

The photograph below shows a West Ham eight-wheeled bogie-car placed in service in 1911. Bogie cars with a greater seating capacity were favoured in many of the larger cities.

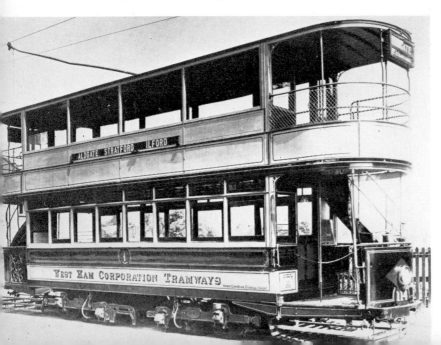

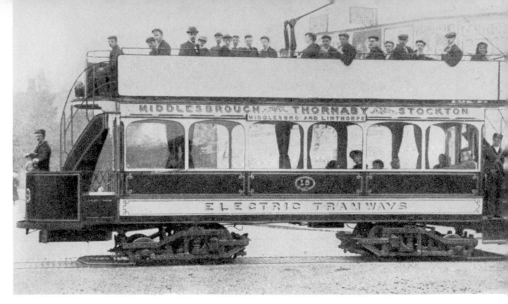

Typical of the capacious double-deck open-topped bogie-cars used in the industrial areas is this Middlesbrough tramcar (*above*) indicating, by the well patronised upper deck and the sparsely inhabited lower saloon, that the hardy northerners much preferred the fresh air on a sunny day. The absence of a canopy over the motorman and his exposed position indicates that he was not given much choice whatever the weather. Although some Edwardian tramcars had the added refinement of curtains downstairs, it was some years before it was thought desirable to construct a canopy over the motorman and a windscreen between him and the elements. One tramway general manager said he thought it was healthier for his motormen to be so exposed. Below is a Bath tramcar of the same period; in this case the motorman is at least under a canopy.

Evolution and World War I

Electric tramways contributed to local scenes by the distinctive variations from a common basic design and by differing liveries in which they were painted. The chocolate and cream trams of the London County Council, the blue and cream trams of Birmingham, the green and cream Black Country tramcars and the grey trams of Gloucester are some examples. In Glasgow the trams extended this characteristic by having their upper decks painted different colours for different routes; round each top deck was painted a band of white, yellow, green, blue or red, exclusive to each route. In a line of trams, waiting to load in the centre of the city, it was easy to pick out one's tramcar quickly. During these years modifications to the original design of tramcars were made. A Liverpool example of the early type of reversed stairs double deck cars (*below*) which prevented the driver having a clear view to his left and also caused top-deck passengers to descend into the path of those leaving the lower saloon, were replaced by the 'direct' type of stair which obviated the previous disadvantages.

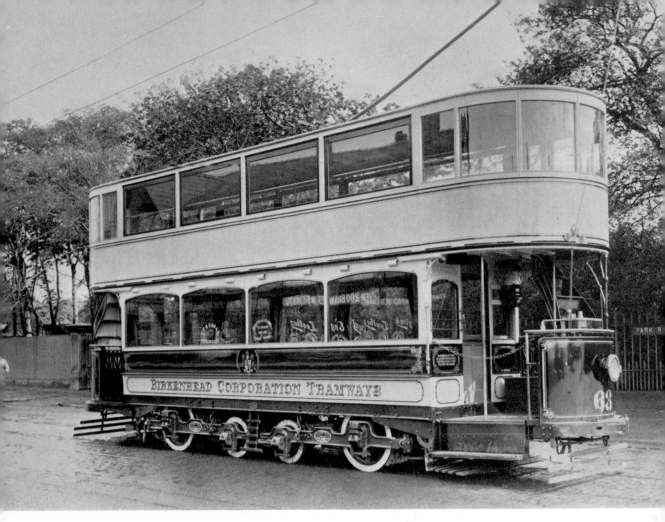

Birkenhead Corporation tramcar No 63 (*above*), a 'low-bridge' car built in 1913, is an illustration of a 'direct' stairway and a totally enclosed upper saloon.

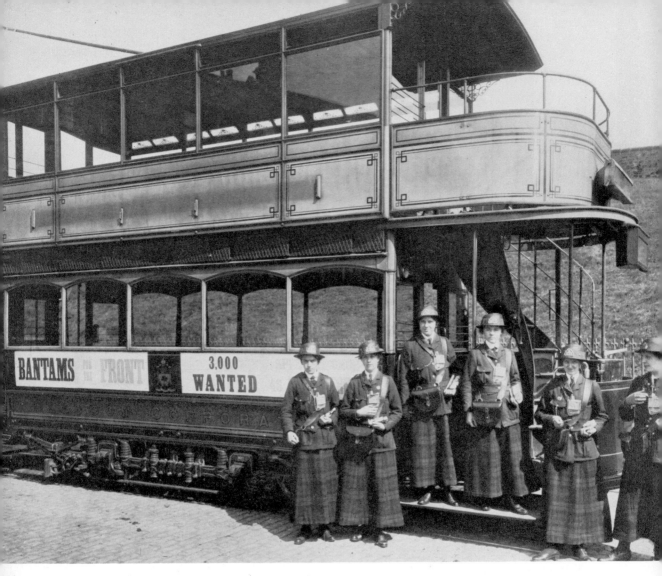

Due to acute shortages of manpower conductresses were extensively employed on tramways, for the first time, in World War I. The Scottish tartan ensures that there is no mistaking the Glasgow tramways and the car itself is a typical example of an early covered-top balcony car. The recruiting poster on the car will be noted with interest.

Later in World War I Glasgow and a few other systems also employed motorwomen in addition to conductresses. The ticketbox with the supply of tickets, cash-pouch, bell-punch and whistle were an integral part of the conductress's equipment while her motorwoman carries her controller handle in one hand and the controller key in the other. The heavy cape must have been a welcome adjunct on a bleak open platform in a Scottish winter (*right*). The trams, including the watercar tram, are held up on Gloucester Cross (*below*) for a platoon of soldiers to march by in 1914. The tramcar on the left-hand track, showing a destination Hucclecote, was extended to Brockworth in 1917 to give a passenger and goods service to a wartime aerodrome and aircraft works, the goods being transferred from the railway in London Road to specially constructed tramway-wagons on the 3ft 6in gauge Gloucester system.

Post War Progress

During the 1914-18 war the electric tramways of the British Isles had rendered great service to the war effort. The coal for their powerstations was home produced and the rolling-stock had withstood the lack of replacements and the continual overloading. A few new tramcars had been built, mainly to convey munition workers and those engaged in the heavy industries necessary for the war. A heavy programme of arrears faced the tramway operators at the conclusion of hostilities. As this war ended so suddenly and no plans for peacetime had been made beforehand, it was not until the 1920s that the delivery of new tramcars became apparent. Also during the post-war years new extensions were undertaken. Birmingham Corporation system exemplifies the enterprise and drive characteristic of the larger undertakings which had had to mark time during the war. The rapid expansion of the city caused a revolutionary policy of extending to the suburbs on 'reserved' track, laid on sleepers, on the median strip which divides the dual carriageway. The narrow Birmingham gauge of 3ft 6in, inherited from the former steam tramways, provided an engineering challenge which Birmingham overcame successfully. Operating both four-wheel cars and eight-wheel bogie-cars with a high degree of utilisation of rolling-stock equipped with air and magnetic track brakes, their extensive fleet was renowned for splendid riding comfort, rapid acceleration, transverse upholstered seating, improved lighting and a minimum of road failures. Visiting foreign tramway engineers frequently expressed their admiration when Birmingham's 15-ton bogie-cars, with their smooth riding qualities, were demonstrated to them, particularly regarding their silent operation on the sleeper-track sections of the system. The illustration below is of one of several batches delivered to Birmingham Corporation during the 1920s, shown running on a 'reserved' section of sleeper-track.

A tramcar at speed on the outskirts of Glasgow, proceeding to Coatbridge on the private track segregated from the roadway though easily accessible to intending passengers. This line was opened in 1922.

This illustration of Dublin's O'Connell Street taken in 1930 shows the extensive track layout of the 5ft 3in gauge of the Dublin United Tramway Company on the wide roadway.

The picture above shows the neat design of a Dearne District Light Railway tramcar with windscreens which were becoming more commonplace as many tramway undertakings began to give greater attention to the comfort of the staff by providing protection against the weather for their motormen. Below is a picture of a Metropolitan tramcar, unvestibuled, although the passengers were well protected by the totally enclosed accommodation on both decks.

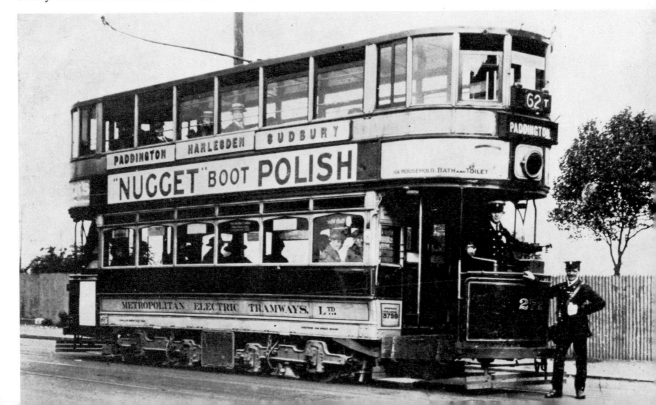

Bradford tramcar No 48 (*above*) and Nottingham car No 99 (*below*) are examples of cars whose enlightened general managers had lowered the incidence of illness amongst their motormen by providing windscreen weather protection. London lagged behind other British cities and towns in enclosing the platform staff behind windscreens as for many years the Metropolitan Police resisted this improvement, long after the advent of safety glass.

Local Characteristics

The regional aspects of electric tramways were determined by the boundaries to which they were confined and also depended upon whether they were financed by the local municipality or were company owned. A number of engineering firms and tramcar builders quickly became geared to electric tramcar construction from 1899 onwards and standard productions were soon available. At the same time, some specifications differed according to local needs which were many and varied. A district with a multiplicity of low railway bridges could not, of course, operate double-deck tramcars, while a large city system with a very intensive passenger-density needed larger capacity cars with more powerful motors. In seaside localities or areas of picturesque scenery, open 'toastrack' tramcars were popular for summer working, while in winter there was a demand for enclosing the upper decks of tramcars already delivered and those on order. A further regional consideration concerned the available capital. The larger municipally owned electric tramways of London, Birmingham, Liverpool, Glasgow, Manchester and similar systems were better placed in modernising their fleets and keeping abreast of the latest improvements than were the company-owned tramways and those of the smaller municipalities.

Illustrated below is a Southport open toastrack tramcar which ran on a circular tour and was very popular with seaside visitors.

A former Bournemouth 3ft 6in gauge open-topped car, one of ten purchased from that corporation by the Llandudno & Colwyn Bay Electric Railway Limited in 1936 (*above*). Open-top cars were also popular with summer visitors but at Llandudno a special rule required passengers to leave the top deck in high wind, as the notice (*below*) indicates.

LLANDUDNO & COLWYN BAY ELECTRIC RAILWAY LTD.

SPECIAL INSTRUCTIONS

During times of high wind and gales the Toll Gate Keeper will observe the velocity of wind as recorded on the indicator dial and will inform the Drivers and Conductors of passing cars if the velocity exceeds 50 miles per hour. Conductors of passing cars will alight from their car and inspect the dial.

At all times when the dial indicates a wind velocity exceeding 50 miles per hour Conductors will request any passengers on the upper deck to transfer to the lower saloon and will not allow any passengers to ride on the top deck until they have again seen the dial or otherwise been informed that the wind velocity has decreased below 50 miles per hour.

Enclosed D.D. Tramcars Nos. 23 and 24. Should the wind velocity exceed 50 Miles per hour, the Drivers will be advised of the fact from the office, to return empty to the Depot until further notice.

BY ORDER

W. G. HAMILTON, A.M.I.E.E.
General Manager

A depot scene of Bath Electric Tramways Limited (*above*) whose system included several very steep hills and one low-bridge route requiring single-deck cars. Another steep hill: a South Metropolitan electric tramcar at the Crystal Palace terminus after ascending the 1 in 9 gradient up Anerley Hill for half a mile (*below*).

London's tramways were characterised by the underground conduit system which avoided the use of poles and overhead wires. Despite this, years of debate elapsed before parliament allowed the trams to cross Westminster Bridge. The above cleverly faked picture was produced by the LCC to support their application; on the right is the site of the present County Hall.

The illustration below shows a typical Bristol scene during rush-hour loading at Old Market. Bristol, early in the electric tramway field, did not adopt top-covered cars, the entire tram fleet remaining open-top until replacement by buses in 1938-41.

Eight miles north-east of Dublin is a promontory into the Irish Sea upon which ran the Hill of Howth tramway, owned and operated by the GNR of Ireland on a 5ft 3in gauge, mainly on a private right-of-way sleeper-track. Opened in 1901, at one point it ran close to a convent and one of the conditions governing its construction was that a high wall should be erected beside the convent to prevent top-deck passengers gazing upon the nuns perambulating the convent grounds in their meditations (*above*).

Southend-on-Sea Corporation's 3ft 6in gauge tramway ran from Leigh-on-Sea along the Boulevards to Thorpe Bay (*below*). The Board of Trade would not allow covered tops on the four-wheel Southend cars, so the later classes were all bogies.

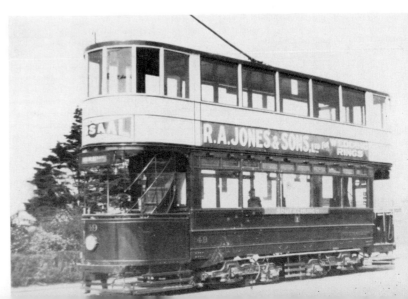

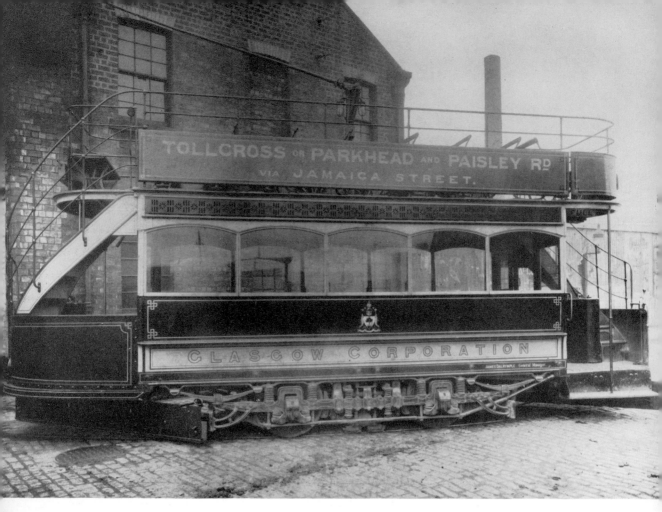

In some cases the oldest tramcars on a system were kept for special work such as snow clearance. The above illustration shows one of the two original 1898 Glasgow double-deckers as later fitted with snow-ploughs. On these two tramcars the controllers were placed behind the stairs, which must have caused the motormen to adopt an awkward stance in driving.

Immingham is situated across the Humber and extensive docks were built there by the Great Central Railway. Due to their awkward accessibility the railway company built an electric tramway in 1911-12 to link the docks with Grimsby. Of 4ft 8½in gauge this tramway, later run by the LNER and British Railways, ran mainly on railway-track where high speeds were maintained on a straight stretch of 5 miles with only four intervening request stops. For this work the cars had to be long single-deck bogie-cars, one of which is shown above outside the depot.

Southampton Corporation tramways were distinguished by special types of low-built double-deck tramcars (*below*) designed to clear the medieval Bargate through which they passed. They had back-to-back seating on the upper decks.

Electrical and Traction Spheres

A constant fascination of electric tramways for youthful enthusiasts was the method of propulsion of the tramcars. Drawing their energy from a central power supply as distinct from a self-contained supply carried on the vehicles, and running on rails, a tramcar always had an air of reliability and comfortable permanency. The central power supply was an overwhelming factor in their cheapness of operation. Except for a small lighting current at night and (in later days) the air compressor for the brakes, electric tramcars only used traction current when they were in motion and, even then, the rolling resistance of a railed vehicle is so low that a considerable distance could be traversed without current when sufficient speed had been attained and a tramcar was 'coasting'. By far the most widespread method of feeding current, at 550 volts dc, to the tramcars was by an overhead trolley-wire, so called because the trolley-pole, swivelling on a mounting on the tramcar with a powerful internal upward spring, carried the trolley-wheel upwards to the trolley-wire. The return circuit was through the negative track rails. The Isle of Thanet tramcar (*below*) illustrates this type of current collection.

There were variants of current collection and, latterly, some used bow-collectors like Birmingham (*top*) and a few used pantographs. Some local authorities objected to overhead trolley-wires as being unsightly and designers 'bent over backwards' to improve this street furniture by ornate cast-iron scroll-work (*centre*). In London objections were so strong that a conduit system of current collection was adopted for 248 miles of tramway. The conduit, very expensive to construct, was a slot between the running rails which gave access to an underground duct through which ran the conductor rails, positive and negative, the current being collected by means of a 'plough' carried by the tramcar, which passed down through the slot to the conductor rails. The illustration below shows a London tramcar from an overhead trolley-wire section arriving at a 'plough-change-pit' and taking on the plough for the conduit section of the tramway.

Two early types of steam-engine driven electric tramway powerstations. The illustrations, both taken in 1895, show (*left*) the generating plant at Laxey, Isle of Man, and (*below*) the first tramway power-station, at Beaconsfield Road, Bristol. The 3ft 8in flywheels were grooved to take ten 1¼in Egyptian cotton ropes driving the three dynamos each with an output of 200 amp at 550 volts at 650 revolutions per minute. One of the new Bristol tramcars can be seen through the doorway leading to the depot.

Still another method of current collection was the 'surface contact' system consisting of a series of metal studs in the centre of the track, placed at intervals. The tramcar carried a long collector plate or 'skate' slightly above the road surface which electro-magnetically attracted the recessed studs, two or more at a time, as the car progressed. Under the roadway in a conduit was a continuous power-cable in contact with the studs. Immediately the tramcar skate broke contact with the studs, by the passage of the car, they returned to their 'dead' position, by the action of a spring, thus becoming de-energised. The only systems using this method were Wolverhampton, Torquay, Mexborough, Lincoln, Hastings and part of London. Surface contact systems were not very successful as occasionally there were cases of springs failing to return a stud to the neutral position thus causing injury to pedestrians and horses through the stud remaining 'live'. The illustration is of the surface contact system in Wolverhampton on their 3ft 6in gauge system. The studs are clearly discernible between the tracks. Eventually all stud contact systems were converted to overhead trolley operation.

Electric tramcars in Great Britain were of two types. The four-wheel single-truck tramcars, which were by far the majority, were employed on the smaller systems and on some of the more lightly loaded routes of cities. The illustration at the top of the opposite page is of a typical four-wheeled truck. Eight-wheeled bogie-cars were mainly used in larger cities and on lines where the traffic warranted their use. Bogie-cars were of two classes of wheel arrangement, the 'maximum-traction' type (*above*) whereby as much of the weight as possible was carried on the larger motor-driven wheels, for adhesion—the pony-wheels, which were not motorised, permitting added length to the tramcar body. The maximum-traction bogie illustrated, with the 70hp motor not yet fitted, is the type with which the 'Feltham' cars of London were equipped. The photograph at the foot of the opposite page is of a much later 'equal-wheel' Maley & Taunton bogie showing the magnetic track brakes and cardan-shaft-drive specially designed for high-speed running, and fitted with resilient wheels containing rubber pads to reduce vibrations, improve passenger comfort and notably decrease noise. These bogies are equipped with two motors for each bogie and in addition to the magnetic track brakes, are provided with rheostatic electric braking and air wheel brakes.

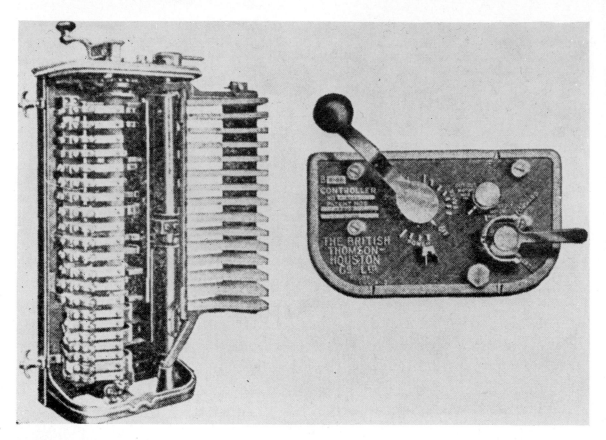

The illustration above of the interior and top-plate of a typical tramcar controller shows the graduated feeding notches on the top-plate. The controller handle is in the 'off' position and, moving forward clockwise, current is fed to the motors to accelerate the tramcar. From the 'off' position anti-clockwise are the electric braking notches whereby rheostatic braking is effected by turning the motors into generators and retarding the car. In addition many tramcars were also equipped with magnetic track brakes operated by current thus supplied by the motors acting as generators. The small 'key' on the right of the controller is locked in the 'off' position and the tramcar immobilised. The 'key' has a 'forward' and a 'reverse' position.

The illustration on the right shows the main principles of a tramcar controller. 1, the handle for operating the main drum, 2. 3, the controller 'key' for rotating the 'reverse' or 'forward' cylinder, 4. The fingers, 9, contact the power cylinder which is separated by the insulating partitions, 5, carried on a movable pole of blow-out magnet, 6. The combined bolt and wrench, 10, fix the blow-out magnet to the pole at 11. Two 'cut-out' switches, 7, are provided to cut out a disabled motor. All cables entering the controller are shown at 8, while 12 is the controller casing. The illustration below is of a modern Maley-Taunton air and magnetic brake interlock mounted on a General Electric controller.

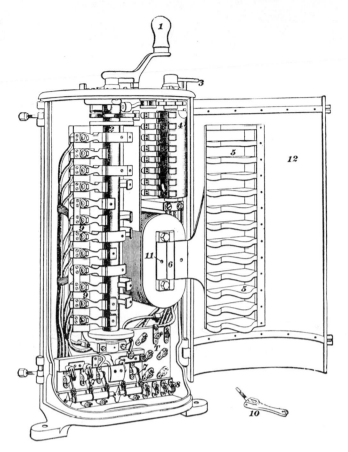

Overhead linesmen repairing a trolley-wire from the top of a tower-wagon. The tower-wagons were constructed to swivel clear to let a tramcar pass, the linesmen then resuming their work. The current could not be switched off and the tramcar service interrupted, consequently these tramway-overhead-linesmen worked on 'live' trolley-wires and stood on an insulated platform.

Social Amenities

The principle of any public transport system is the carriage of passengers in bulk at cheap rates. Only by a strict regard for this precept will its existence be justified or its continued success be possible. The electric tramcars of Great Britain fulfilled this role to a degree which has still not been reached since their demise. Furthermore, in addition to swift acceleration and braking they were clean, efficient and had the advantage of not polluting the atmosphere of the streets with heavy diesel fumes.

Fares at remarkably cheap rates had always been the attraction for tramcar passengers, and in 1902 passengers in Glasgow travelled four stages, approximately $2\frac{1}{4}$ miles, for their penny. Other towns had equally cheap fares but probably the cheapest ever were those of the London County Council Tramways. Their '2d All the Way' tickets between the hours of 10am and 4pm ensured that, in off-peak traffic hours, housewives could shop far afield and the tramcars were always well loaded, instead of running practically empty during mid-day. Another LCC bargain was the '1/- All Day Ticket' whereby it was possible to travel anywhere on the LCC's 160 miles of electric tramways for 24 hours (including the 'all-night' services) changing cars at will (*below*).

A London 'All-Night' service car at Tooting Broadway. The 'All-Night Trams' provided a reliable and efficient passenger transport service mainly at half-hourly intervals throughout the night, greatly appreciated and used by newspaper staffs, railway staffs, bakers, nurses and other shift workers.

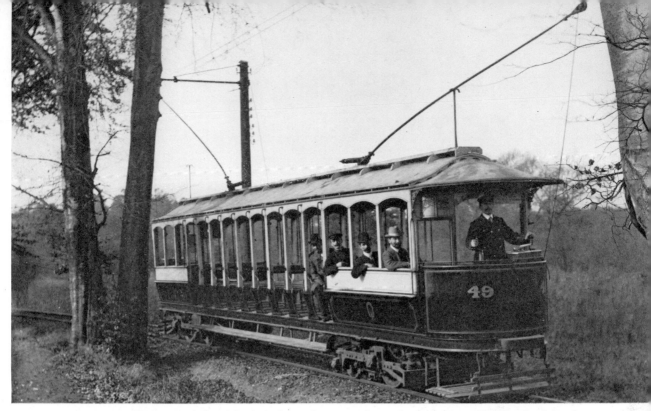

Tramcars also provided townsfolk with their favourite excursions. A tramway well patronised in the summer was the 3ft 6in gauge light railway operated by the Dudley Stourbridge & District Electric Traction Company Limited in the Midlands. Starting at Colburnbrook, near Stourbridge, the tramway ran through the streets for the first mile until it reached the Ridge Top at Wollaston. At this point the tramway forsook the roadway and ran on its own private reservation, on sleeper-tracks, at the side of the road, crossing the highway again at the Stewponey Inn at the junction of the Stourbridge-Bridgnorth and Kidderminster-Wolverhampton roads. From this stage it resumed its sleeper-track through the fields to Kinver, a renowned beauty-spot known as 'the Switzerland of the Midlands' and the mecca of so many visitors out for a day's trip from the Black Country. The illustration above shows an open type summer car on a picturesque stretch of the light railway, while the scene below is also a bogie-car adaptable for summer and winter use, at Kinver terminus. The milk-churns are awaiting collection by the 'Tramway Parcels Express', another service rendered by the light railway for this rural community.

An amenity provided by electric tramways was the provision of snowploughs. As the tracks had to be kept clear of snow for their own vehicles, the tramways rapidly cleared accumulating snow, a service which benefited other road-users as well, at no cost to the local rates. The illustration above shows a Birmingham Corporation tramcar, on a central tramway reservation, fitted with snowploughs. At the first sign of snow, the detachable lifeguards were removed and the ploughs were fitted to a proportion of tram-cars sufficient to keep the tracks clear for all cars. On smaller systems, special snowplough cars were used. The electric tramcar had the great advantage in that it maintained normal speeds when the tracks had been cleared of snow, as it could not skid on snow or ice. In addition it was equipped with rail-sanding pipes in front of the wheels, operated by the motorman, to assist adhesion and braking.

Flooded roadways did not always deter the tramcars from getting their passengers to their destinations. The scene below, in North London, shows two 'Feltham' type tramcars nearly waterborne.

Some Urban Services

To the city-dweller the dense and complex service, with a short headway between tramcars, was a boon. For many years, although no standing passengers were allowed on the upper decks of tramcars, there was practically no limit to the number carried on the lower decks. This gave rise to many humorous stories about 'the last car at night from the terminus' and, even when apparently full, the capacity of the tramcar for crowding in even more standing passengers was remarkable. Some London tramcars designed to carry seventy-four seated passengers on both decks have been known to contain over a hundred passengers when a football ground emptied or the theatres turned out late at night. On New Year's Eve 1953, the last tramcar at night in Hope Street, Glasgow was stopped by an inspector and found to have 106 passengers aboard! But with powerful brakes and automatic lifeguards for the protection of errant pedestrians the tramcar was a very safe form of transport. Their accident rate was extremely low in relation to the extensive mileage traversed and the large number of passengers carried. Robustly built, their sound construction amazed even the maintenance staffs. In 1962 when the electric tramcars ended well over half-a-century's honourable service in Glasgow, serviceable tramcars over sixty years old were still to be seen. Quite true they had been re-motored, had had air-brakes fitted and other modern modifications but it says much for the original bodywork construction that they were still in service. In contrast it is worth recording that the effective life of a motorbus is regarded as fifteen to twenty years. A characteristic urban service, the Potteries Electric Traction Company covered the 'Five Towns' immortalised by Arnold Bennett. The actual area of the undertaking was ongton, Fenton, Stoke, Hanley, Burslem, Tunstall, Newcastle-under-Lyme, Wolstanton, Silverdale and Chesterton, the 4ft gauge lines serving the densely populated industrial district. The local railway company complained that it had lost 800,000 passengers to the tramway during the first year of its operation, in 1899. In 1902 the PET carried 14,428,048 passengers in their fleet of 105 tramcars, a preponderance of large bogie-cars and a number of four-wheel ones, all single deck. The worst hazard of the company was subsidence in the mining area necessitating costly track maintenance. In addition the company paid £10,000 a year in rates for roadways built and maintained by themselves! Despite all this, the efficient system and the 30 miles of line made a profit.

The largest electric tramway undertaking in the North East was the extensive network of Newcastle-on-Tyne Corporation, its 50 route miles of 4ft 8½in gauge track with over 300 cars, single and double deck, both four and eight-wheel types, operating in Newburn, Westerhope, Gosforth, Longbenton and Wallsend. It also provided £100,000 to carry the lines across the High Level and New Tyne bridges, giving Newcastle and Gateshead extensive cross-river services. The Tyneside Tramways and Tramroads Company, connecting Wallsend-on-Tyne with North Shields and Gosforth, owned 11 route miles in that area with running powers over 5 miles of the corporation's lines, while south of the Tyne, the Gateshead & District Tramways Company, owning 12½ miles of route, enjoyed a similar facility, providing a joint service between Newcastle and Gateshead termini with 67 tramcars, 36 single-deck and the rest double deck.

In the North West, the adjoining towns of Manchester and Salford provided an interesting example of the advantages of through running on their 4ft 8½in gauge systems. Manchester's 123 route miles operated by 950 cars was the third largest in Great Britain, and Salford's 40 miles of tramway with 230 cars augmented this vast urban service. In addition, cars belonging to five neighbouring corporations and two companies exercised running powers into Manchester. It was a colourful sight to see the cars of different liveries intermingling, for nowhere else in the country could cars belonging to so many operators be seen running on the same tracks, Manchester being unique as the centre of a large urban network comprising over 300 miles of route.

An artist's impression of a well-patronised last tramcar in Glasgow, late at night.

Holborn tramway station on the Kingsway subway, which ran through from the Embankment to Southampton Row. A very well-patronised route because the subway avoided congested streets.

A tramcar descending the gradient and entering the Kingsway subway at Southampton Row, London from which it ran underground, emerging on the Victoria Embankment. A slum area of London was cleared by the LCC and the handsome thoroughfares of Kingsway and Aldwych were formed, the opportunity being taken to construct a tramway subway—the works being carried out simultaneously and completed in 1908—for single-deck tramcars which carried 200,000 passengers a week, providing a service from 5am to nearly 1am. As the tramway along Victoria Embankment via Westminster Bridge had already been opened, the tramways north and south of the Thames were linked for the first time. The subway was temporarily closed in 1930 for reconstruction to take double-deck cars and reopened with them in 1931, providing over 100 per cent increase in seating capacity with through running over a wider area.

A heavily loaded LCC Class E/1 tramcar hauling an equally heavily loaded trailer on 13 December 1913. The trellis expanding-type protection between the two vehicles, insisted on by the Board of Trade, also prevented more youthful and agile passengers taking a short cut over the tow-bar between the two vehicles.

Although widely used on the continent with single-deck tramcars, trailer-cars were frowned on by the authorities in Great Britain. In the early years of electric traction some systems, notably Bristol, Dover, Grimsby, the Potteries and Southampton gave trailers a trial. Due to intensive traffic requirements, London County Council experimented with trailers in 1911, and 158 were purchased in the early months of World War I. They helped to overcome the acute manpower shortage during that period as trailers only needed a conductor and required little maintenance. Because of curves and gradients their use was restricted to South London. The LCC trailers met Board of Trade requirements of an automatic brake which applied itself should a trailer break loose but it was found that, due to shunting movements at termini, they were an operating hindrance and continual complaints from the police resulted in their withdrawal in 1922-3. The Ministry of Transport seems to have relented in recent years as modern lightweight trailers have been sanctioned, to be towed by single-deck tramcars, and are now in use at Blackpool where there are no shunting problems, the termini being provided with turning-circles.

In comparison with the extensive mileage traversed and the vast networks covered, electric tramcar accidents were extremely rare and photographs of them accordingly rarer still. The illustration below is of a London United tramcar which derailed at Kingston-on-Thames, obstructing the roadway and delaying traffic. The advertisement panel for the play *Gay Bohemia* seems to have been taken too literally by the tramcar.

A plough-change-pit in Mile End Road, London, looking east. The outward bound tramcars shed their ploughs at these change-pits, proceeding to the terminus on the overhead trolley-wire system. The ploughs were guided through the conduit junction and held ready for city-bound cars using the conduit system when these cars took on the ploughs. The 'ploughman' can be seen guiding the plough with his fork into the plough-channels of a city-bound car.

The last car built for Birmingham Corporation's extensive 3ft 6in gauge system. It had an experimental lightweight body and seating for sixty passengers. All the corporation's cars were painted in a neat and dignified livery of dark blue and primrose with gold lining and shaded numerals. The car shown above is at Pebble Mill Road and the tramway clock was operated by motormen to 'clock-in' the arrival of cars at this point (clock 29), a feature of the Birmingham system.

Edinburgh's renowned Princes Street was traversed by a fleet of very modern covered-top four-wheeled tramcars on 4ft 8½in gauge. Their dark red livery was distinctive and, as befitted the City and Royal Burgh of Edinburgh, their electric tramcars were very sedate, well-upholstered and smooth riding (*below*).

One of the highest-density electric tramway services in Great Britain: a scene at Westminster Embankment, London. The conduit tramway-tracks were immediately adjoining the wide Thames-side pavement on the side of the motor carriageway.

A night depot scene at Dundee (*above*), a city which always maintained its tramcar fleet in excellent condition. The corporation, which had always owned the tracks even when horse-operated by a company, took them over and electrified them at the beginning of the century.

North of Dundee a most progressive Aberdeen Corporation provided a service with an enviable reputation for the high standard of maintenance; their King Street works is illustrated below.

The extensive Manchester Corporation 4ft 8½in gauge system of bogie and four-wheeled tramcars was a tramway enthusiast's paradise. In addition to its enclosed double-deck cars, its fleet included just over sixty single-deck fast bogie-cars for use on the low-bridge routes of Pottery Lane and Stanley Grove. In 1930 a number of high-speed four-wheel 'Pilcher' cars (so called after the then general manager) were introduced, incorporating many new features including two 50hp motors, upholstered seats throughout and deep domed roofs painted silver. The bodies of the 'Pilchers' (*above*) were constructed at the corporation's Hyde Road works. Below is an illustration of the extensive main depot at Hyde Road.

Special Duty Tramcars

The primary role of electric tramways to provide an efficient and cheap passenger transport system was sustained by a number of maintenance tramcars, stores-van tramcars (for moving equipment between central stores and depots), water-cars and, on some systems, a useful source of revenue was the carriage of parcels and goods. One type of maintenance service tramcar was the heavy wheel-carrier (*below*) of London, shown running on a conduit section of the tramway, carrying tramcar wheels before and after re-tyring to and from the works and the various depots.

An LCC stores van (*above*). Some of these miscellaneous vehicles were reconstructed from previous passenger cars.

A Leeds rail-grinder, towing an equipment-trailer (*below*). The grinding-wheels were used mostly at night for levelling rail corrugations in the track. Rail-welding was also done at night to avoid interrupting the passenger service.

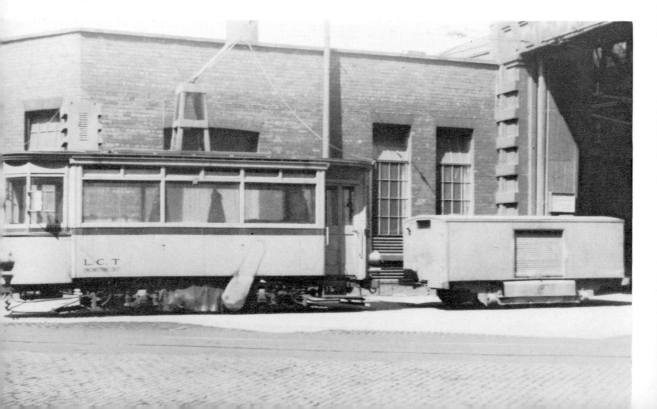

Tramcars rarely seen by the public because they usually operated at night when no passenger cars were running were the engineering cars. Above is an illustration of a comprehensively equipped one belonging to Blackpool Corporation. This car not only includes a tower-wagon for use on the Light Railway section of the system where road tower-wagons could not operate, but also has a diesel generator inside in order to drive under its own power when overhead trolley-wires are 'dead', either through an emergency or at night.

Huddersfield Corporation, in addition to their passenger tramcars, conducted a profitable coal-transport service between the LNW Railway Hillhouse sidings and some local mills. The illustration below shows a specially built tramway-coal-truck of which two were used, powered by two 45hp motors.

Above is illustrated a tramway parcels-express car towing a goods truck (familiary known as the 'TPE') on the extensive 3ft 6in gauge company-owned system of the Midlands. This lucrative side of the tramway system was remarkably efficient and parcels and goods collected at a central point (usually a local shop with the 'TPE' sign prominently displayed outside) would be delivered the same day very many miles away. The milk-churns from the rural Kinver Light Railway were also distributed over a wide area by this service.

In the early 1900s before tar-macadam roads became general, only the tramways were paved with setts between the rails and extending to 18in each side of the tracks. The remainder of the roadways consisted of compacting stone, broken small and grouted in with sand and water. Such poor surfaces caused excessive dust on hot windy days, accentuated by the early motorcars whose passage was accompanied by large clouds of following dust, smothering and discomforting pedestrians. Many corporations included in their tramcar fleets a water-car, used for washing the accumulated dust from the grooved tracks to assist better electrical conductivity in exceptionally dry weather. The illustration at the top of the next page shows one of this type of vehicle, in Aberdeen, equipped additionally with sprinklers to dampen down the dust over a wider area. The tanks of the water-cars were replenished from water-columns situated at intervals on the pavements, which were also used to replenish horsedrawn water-carts on roads where the tramways did not run. This particular Aberdeen water-car could also be fitted with a detachable snowplough and was so used, with the water-tank filled to capacity to give the necessary added adhesion for snowplough working, in this most northerly town tramway in the British Isles.

Below, a London snowbroom tramcar preceding a passenger car. Underneath the platform a revolving brush was mounted, at an angle, which swept the snow from the offside to the nearside, clearing the tracks.

Illuminated tramcars were frequently used for special events or appeals. The picture above is of a Bristol tramcar decorated to help raise money for a children's fund.

Tramcars were available for private hire. The decorated Colchester tramcar above took guests from the North Station to the High Street for the wedding and reception of a local nurseryman's daughter in 1905.

Although popular on the continent, advertisement tramcars were not very often used in Great Britain. The one shown on the right toured the city of Glasgow to give publicity to an exhibition.

A Typical Small System

The local characteristics of the many town electric tramway systems of Great Britain are best seen by taking the example of one small system (in contrast with London, Birmingham, Glasgow, Liverpool, Manchester and other large cities) and glancing at its history. That of Reading Corporation was typical of the civic pride and efficiency of its time. During the end of the nineteenth century the population of Reading had grown to 70,000 and a Bill authorising the construction of electric tramways, after the usual delays by objectors, received Royal Assent on 30 July 1900. For historical reasons the Reading system was laid to the non-standard gauge of 4ft, previously used by the horse trams. The illustration below is of a Reading Corporation tramcar, en route from the makers on a railway wagon, to be delivered at the inception of the system.

The depot and powerstation were erected in Mill Lane. The powerstation was a model of its kind, always maintained in immaculate condition, and the first rolling-stock consisted of thirty four-wheeled tramcars supplied by the renowned tramcar-builders Dick Kerr & Company Limited of Preston. The cars were 27ft long seating twenty-two passengers inside and twenty-eight on the upper deck, carried on Brill 21E type trucks with two 25hp motors.

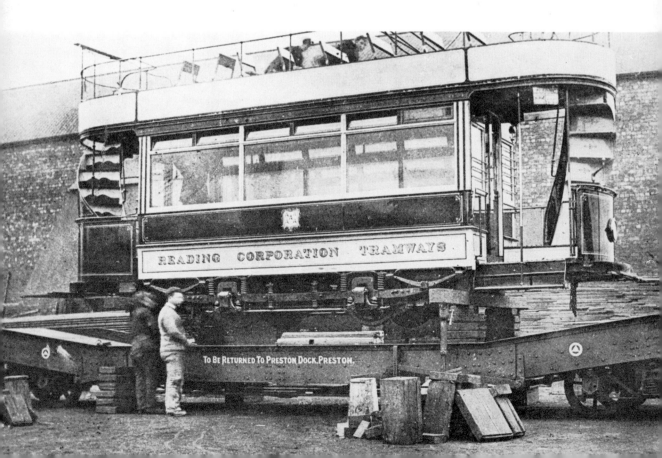

The livery was crimson lake with cream rocker-panels, the imposing Reading Corporation crest being on the waist-panel. The total capital expenditure for installing the electric tramway system in Reading was £223,000 and, after the Board of Trade inspection on 14 July 1903, the ceremonial opening took place on 22 July 1903, the Mayor, Alderman A. H. Bull, driving the first car. The Oxford Road-Wokingham Road was the 'main line' and the lesser subsidiary routes leading to the centre of the town were regarded as feeder routes. The illustration above shows Car No 23 at Wokingham Road terminus. A peculiarity of Reading tramcars was a curved bar in front of the motorman.

The only addition to Reading's tramcar fleet during its whole existence was made in 1904 by the purchase of six bogie-cars and a water-car-cum-snowplough. The bogie-cars were 33ft 6in long seating thirty passengers inside and forty on the top deck. They were powered by two 35hp motors and also supplied by Dick Kerr & Company Limited. The first financial year of operation resulted in a net profit of £2,923 which remained fairly constant, rising steadily to a net profit of £3,390 in 1908-9 and £4,420 in 1914 before World War I. To regard these figures in correct perspective for the period it should be realised that coal was 9s 3d a ton, motormen's overcoats 20s 6d each, trousers 8s 10d a pair and peaked caps 2s 8d each. The highest paid motormen earned 6d an hour and the highest paid conductors 5d an hour for a basic week of 65 hours.

A process of rebuilding the fleet was embarked on from 1920 onwards, the four-wheel cars being fitted with four-window bodies instead of the previous three, and direct quarter-turn stairs in place of the reversed type (illustrated on page 72) which impeded the motorman's vision to his left. It was not until 1925 that vestibuled ends were tried, and even then only thirteen cars were so equipped. The illustration below shows tramcar No 9 at London Road terminus after being vestibuled.

In 1923 a track re-laying programme commenced and was spread over the next six years. Throughout the life of Reading electric tramways, although the entire fleet consisted of double-deck cars they could not be equipped with top-covers for the protection of passengers because of the low-arched railway bridge on the main line of the tramway at Oxford Road. The illustration above of car No 21 with the notice on the bridge requesting passengers to remain seated, also shows the short single-track section to give tram-cars the necessary clearance under the bridge. For safety reasons the trolley-wires have also been positioned away from the upper-decks of the cars. Reading tramcars were always noted for their immaculate condition and high standard of maintenance. They were repainted every two years in numerical sequence; immediately car No 36 was finished, car No 1's turn was due.

In his report for 1929-30, the last year when the entire tramway was in operation before the commencement of the erosion by motorbuses, the Reading general manager recorded tramcar passengers as totalling 12,225,100, an increase of 177,052 on the previous year. Traffic receipts were £76,226, representing 19.33 pence per car mile; passengers carried equalled 151 journeys per head of the population; during early morning a tramcar service operated from the Oxford Road terminus with a headway of two minutes. In retrospect the general manager's conclusions are illuminating when he relates that the daily average service of 23 tramcars operating over 7 miles of streets carried over 12 million passengers while the 20 omnibuses in daily use over 25 miles of streets conveyed 4¾ million passengers in the same period. He sums up by expressing the hope that the comparison will give some idea of the large number of buses which would be required to carry the number of passengers carried by the tramcars, and concludes by warning his committee of the conditions of traffic congestion should buses be substituted for tramcars. The warning was unheeded, however, as this proved to be the zenith year of electric tramways in Reading and tramway abandonments commenced from this date culminating in final closure on 30 May 1939. The illustration above shows bogie-car No 36 awaiting scrapping on a siding, a sad valediction to a most efficient, reliable and prosperous system.

The Crisis Years

During the mid-1920s the motorbus became a serious competitor of electric tramways, although it had nothing like the same passenger-carrying capacity at that time. Indeed, to this day, no motorbus has yet been produced to seat 106 passengers as did the discarded tramcars of the Swansea & Mumbles line, or the 94 seated passengers which are still carried on the splendid double-deck Blackpool tramcars. Prior to the 1920s the motorbus, with its solid tyres, jolted its passengers on their uncomfortable journeys to the accompaniment of excessive noise and pungent fumes. The first of these disadvantages was removed by the new pneumatic tyres for buses; the engine roar and acrid fumes remain to this day. Below is an illustration of two Swansea & Mumbles high-capacity tramcars built by the Brush Electrical Engineering Company of Loughborough and introduced on that line in 1929. The largest electrically-driven tramcars built for service in these islands, for rush-hour service they could be coupled in pairs and driven as a multiple-unit train from either end, carrying 212 seated passengers. Running on a segregated 'reserved' track for just over 5 miles, with pantograph current collection, the passenger figures for 1945 reached the unprecedented number of 4,995,000 carried on a total fleet of only thirteen tramcars.

Some of the smaller company-owned systems also put up a fight against the buses which were using their paved and maintained roadway on their routes. The Birmingham & Midland Tramways Joint Committee, responsible for the company-owned tramways of the Black Country, changed their policy of partly double-deck open-topped cars and some single-deck cars to a fleet of mainly single-deck totally enclosed tramcars (with the exception of those running into Birmingham). After purchasing their original fleet from the usual builders, they set up their own works at Tividale, near Dudley, where they built the new fleet. Below is an illustration of a Tividale-built tramcar on their Dudley-Stourbridge service in 1930.

Amazingly and quite inexplicably many local authorities granted bus licences for their area allowing unfair competition with the electric tramways which were compelled, by law, to maintain the major part of the road surfaces of their routes. Buses operated to no such disadvantages as they merely paid, in comparison, a relatively small road tax none of which accrued to the tramway undertakings for road maintenance. The company-owned tramways were the first to suffer under this penal system which parliament refused to modify. Even so, in 1927 there were still over 14,000 tramcars in Great Britain, of which 12,000 were municipally owned. Some tramways, mostly company-owned, were abandoned during the 1920-30 period but the remainder did not take the bus competition lying down. Improvements in the shape of discarding the previous hard longitudinal seating in favour of upholstered transverse seats in the lower saloon, with leather upholstery in the upper saloon, were adopted as standard on some systems. The illustration above of the lower saloon interior of a London tramcar indicates the types of improvement.

An entirely revolutionary design of tramcar incorporating many new features—the renowned 'Feltham' tramcar—was put into service in north London in February 1931. One hundred of these splendid tramcars were built, fifty-four for the Metropolitan Electric Tramways and forty-six for London United Tramways, at a cost of £3,420 each, a remarkably low figure for such admirable vehicles which were 40ft in length and very spacious.

Further tramcar improvements including more powerful motors, quicker acceleration and more powerful braking, enclosed platforms for the crews or separate driving compartments, silent gears, streamlined bodywork and more attractive liveries were introduced. Additionally the tramcars could always compete favourably with buses by their remarkably cheap fares which held bus competition in check for a long time. The 'Feltham' tramcars with their front exits had the advantage of considerably speeding up the service by facilitating rapid loading and unloading. Equipped with roller-bearings, very powerful motors, air and magnetic track brakes interconnected to the wheel brakes, the smooth riding of these cars was greatly appreciated by Londoners. When the conversion to trolley-buses took place in north London in 1938 the 'Felthams' were transferred to south London and remained in service there until the abandonment of London's tramways in 1952, when the remaining ninety were sold to Leeds tramways, giving sterling service there until the Leeds abandonment in 1959.

Illustrated below is the Welsh answer to bus competition, an improved type of Swansea tramcar.

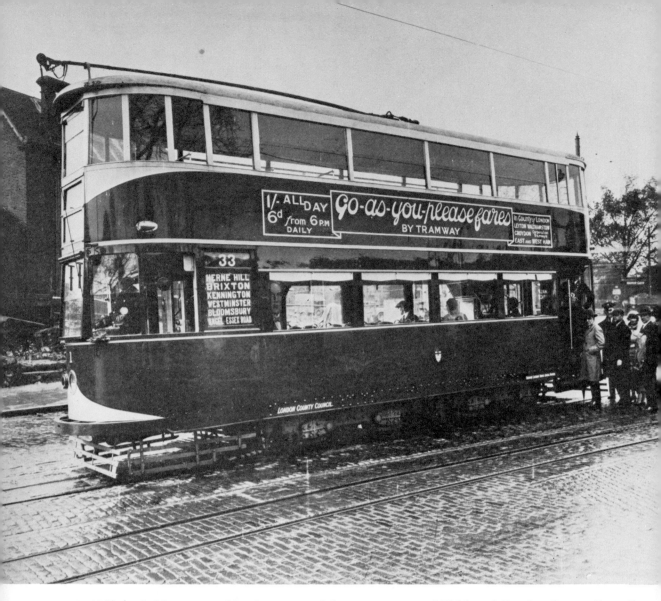

In 1932, probably prompted by the success of the company-owned 'Felthams', London County Council constructed at their Charlton works the prototype of what was intended to be a fleet of luxury tramcars. This car (*above*), known as the 'Blue Car', was renowned for the luxury of its appointments. Painted mainly in blue livery its seating was also in blue upholstery. The motorman had a fully enclosed cab and, being numbered '1', it was said to presage a new fleet of 500 similar tramcars which, due to a change of policy when London Transport took over, never materialised.

The World War II Scene

In 1939 those cities which had retained their electric tramcar services and resisted the motorbus fever had real cause to be thankful, for in the adverse conditions to be faced during the ensuing $5\frac{1}{2}$ years the tramcar really came into its own. Unlike the bus which relied on imported fuel, the remaining tramways were dependent upon coal mined in Great Britain. Again, unlike the bus, the tramcars did not suffer from the blacked-out streets and very restricted vehicle and street lighting, for the tracks were a reliable and safe guide to their destinations. Towns which had abandoned their tramways also had to endure the reduced bus services which, in many cases, terminated at nine o'clock in the evenings in addition to providing far fewer buses. In the air raids it was remarkable how comparatively quickly tramway services were restored, after necessary repairs, having regard to the extensive damage suffered to tracks and overhead trolley-wires. In common with the rest of the country the tramways suffered casualties and the photograph below shows Bedminster depot, Bristol after the blitz of 3-4 January 1941.

Some cities employed women drivers. Considering the weight of a tramcar (anything up to 20 tons), this demonstrates the ease with which such a vehicle can be controlled by air, regenerative, and magnetic track brakes. In February 1941, Glasgow trained the first group of twenty-six motorwomen, and this number was increased as the war dragged on. Above is a Glasgow motorwoman in 1942. By her happy smile, seen in the passenger-mirror above her, she is obviously well in control and enjoying tramcar driving.

The illustration below is of a 'Feltham' tramcar in wartime London showing the windows sealed with adhesive cloth netting as a precaution against bomb-blast shattering them. The diamond-shaped apertures were to enable passengers to identify their whereabouts. The protective netting was not affixed to the driver's screen nor the front upper-saloon windows as these were of splinterproof glass. The scored side-panels and some missing side lifeguard slats show how hard-pressed were the heavily reduced wartime maintenance staff in their endeavours to keep the fleet in service. Pre-war tramcars, of all systems, were always maintained in immaculate condition as evidence of civic pride.

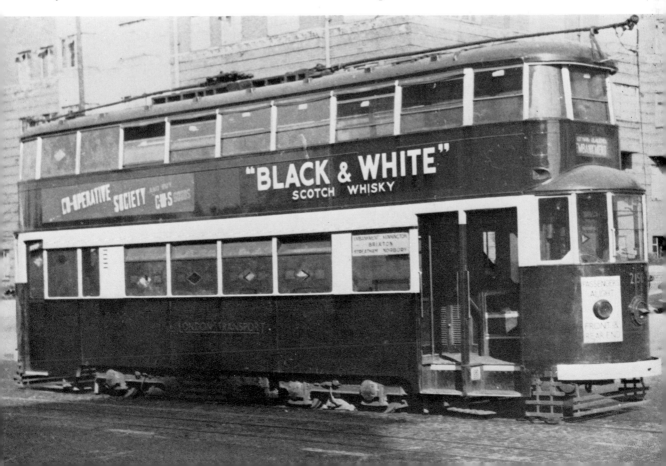

Another casualty, a tramcar which took a direct hit in Nelson Street, Glasgow with heavy casualties during the Clydeside blitz on 14 March 1941. Incredibly this tramcar was subsequently rebuilt at Glasgow Corporation's renowned Coplawhill works and put back into service.

A post-war scene at the Elephant and Castle, London (*above*), the wrecked buildings illustrating the extent of wartime damage with which the tramcars had to contend to maintain the service. This picture, taken on 11 September 1946, shows three 'Felthams' and two London standard cars, with their wartime protective window-gauze removed. It indicates at this busy junction how well the tracks survived such a long period of restricted maintenance with only occasional 'first aid' and blitz repairs.

Arrears and Some Progress

At the conclusion of hostilities a very heavy programme of maintenance both in their trackwork and in their fleets faced electric-tramway operators. One anxiety, which had no relation to the tramcar versus motorbus controversy, was the continuous rise in costs, accentuated by the fact that in the major cities, tramways had borne the brunt of passenger transportation under appallingly adverse conditions. This situation left municipalities and transport boards with an unenviable problem: whether to rehabilitate their tramways or decide on replacement buses. While in the South they decided on the latter course, it seemed as though Glasgow, Birmingham, Liverpool, Leeds and Sheffield, impressed by the reliability and yeoman service rendered by the tramcars in the war effort, would remain faithful to their tramcars, carry out the necessary renewals and, in some cases, expand their services. Sheffield, as befitted the home of the steel industry, took great pride in its efficient and well-maintained tramway system. The illustration below is one of their modern post-war tramcars at Beauchief. Sheffield tramways were remarkable for their high-capacity cars on four-wheel trucks as the terrain required special braking systems which could not easily be fitted to bogie-cars.

In the post-war years London soldiered on with their pre-war tramcars (*above*), pursuing a policy of 'make-do and mend' until the final bus take-over in 1952, a tribute to the robustly built tramcars and soundly constructed tracks and electrical equipment which, after five and a half years of scantily maintained war service, were called on for another seven years' wear until the buses were built. The illustration is of two of the always well patronised Victoria Embankment tramcars on a heavily loaded route.

In their fleet replacement programme Glasgow designed an entirely new streamlined tramcar incorporating many fresh and interesting features. Built at their Coplawhill works, the first of these striking vehicles was put into service in 1948 and between then and 1952 a hundred of these new and improved tramcars were built. The photograph above is of a post-war 'Cunarder' bogie type tramcar, strikingly impressive in its gleaming dominant orange livery.

Liverpool had a flying start in overtaking their wartime arrears as, in 1934, the decision to modernise their tramcar fleet had been taken. From 1935 to 1942 over 200 new bogie-cars, seating seventy-eight passengers, and 100 four-wheeled cars, seating seventy passengers were built at their Edge Lane works on EMB and Maley & Taunton trucks. The illustration below is of a Liverpool four-wheel car.

An impressive Liverpool bogie streamlined tramcar No 153, mounted on EMB lightweight bogies, when new in 1937. The car is shown on a section of 'reserved' track segregated from the carriageway. The glistening olive-green livery of the Liverpool fleet was extremely attractive.

One of the most remarkable post-war abandonment policies was that of Aberdeen. Four excellent modern double-deck tramcars were constructed in 1940 followed by another twenty after the war, up to 1949. Two were four-wheeled cars and the remaining twenty-two were bogie-cars with central entrances and high passenger capacity, designed to run on the wide trunk road of the Bridge of Dee to Bridge of Don route. Despite these recent additions of streamlined cars to an existing reliable fleet, the extravagant decision to abandon the tramways of Aberdeen was taken and the last tramcar ran on 3 May 1958. The whole of the fleet was scrapped, including the foregoing splendid tramcars not ten years old. The modern four-wheel Aberdeen tramcars are illustrated above.

Mainly Valedictory and in Retrospect

An intriguing aspect of the electric tramways of Great Britain, as with all rail traction in these islands, was the extraordinary vigilance of parliament to ensure in meticulous detail the safety of the passengers and, indeed, of other road users. It is a sobering thought to reflect upon what our Victorian and Edwardian forefathers would have done faced with the present road holocaust. Certainly, in their day, they held human life in far higher esteem than it is held in this day and age. In no comparable sphere is this evidenced more precisely than in the regulations governing the operation of electric tramways. Not only were they multitudinous but, in those days, an ever watchful Board of Trade (latterly the Ministry of Transport) retained an adequate body of inspectors to see that they were obeyed to the letter. Although it is not possible to examine all the vast quantity of safety precautions to which electric tramways were subjected, a few interesting ones, visible to the public, will give an indication of the care taken. All the tramcars illustrated in this book were equipped with lifeguards below the driver's platform, a few inches above rail-level. By law an approved pattern lifeguard had to be fitted to every tramcar, designed to pick up without serious injury any person falling in front of a moving car. Mainly known as the 'gate-and-tray-trigger-type' lifeguard, they did not depend for operation on any action of the driver but were entirely automatic. When pushed back by an obstruction, the 'gate' automatically actuated the 'tray' which fell on the roadway by the 'trigger' action, preventing the wheels from injuring the victim. The 'tray' was re-set afterwards by the driver depressing a platform pedal. No similar device is provided on motorbuses, coaches or motorcars. The illustration of the Swansea single-deck bogie-car below clearly shows this protective device.

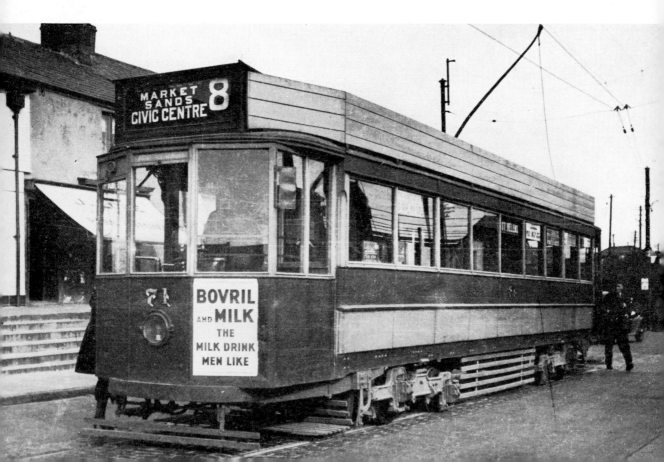

A familiar British street scene in the early twentieth century. This could be a cold job before the days of windscreens and even the capes provided could not prevent hoar-frost on the motorman's eyebrows and (if he had one) moustache, in icy weather.

How they handled the crowds in 1932: a scene at Victoria terminus, London showing eager passengers boarding the tramcars from both platforms. Most London tramcars were dual-equipped for overhead and conduit current collection but the car in front is equipped for conduit track only as its roof has no trolley-poles.

Again, by law, the trolley-heads, containing the trolley-wheels, were required to be affixed to the trolley-boom by a detachable sleeve which, following a dewirement, would immediately detach to prevent entanglement with the span-wire construction, a procedure designed to prevent trolley-wires being brought down. An interesting photograph (*below*) taken in 1907, emphasises the concern of the Board of Trade for safety standards. Trials were carried out by the Municipal Tramways Association to 'investigate the whole subject of tramcar brakes, sanding arrangements etc' by a special committee. Leeds was chosen for the trials and many designs of brakes were tested. They were conducted by the late Mr A. W. Maley, then Assistant Engineer to Leeds Corporation (second from right in the foreground) who afterwards founded the renowned tramcar equipment firm of Maley & Taunton.

(*left*) The ease of control of an electric tramcar is exemplified by this Glasgow motorwoman, a picture taken in 1950 showing the young girl driver of a modern post-war 'Coronation-type' double-deck bogie-car powered by four 35hp motors. The finger-tip control of rapid acceleration and impressive deceleration needs no emphasis with such a confident lady in charge.

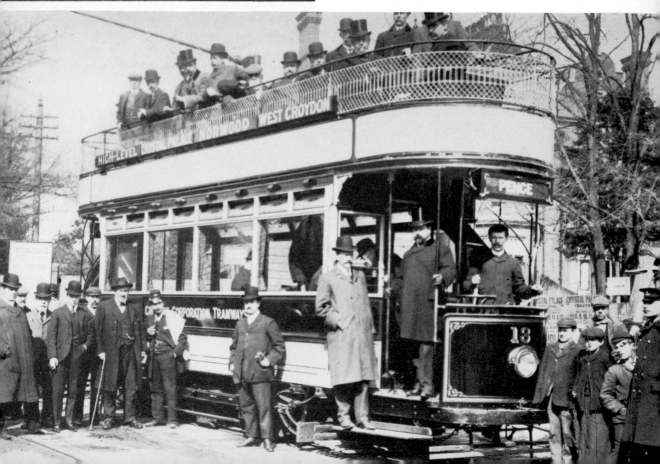

All electric-tramway routes had to be inspected by a Board of Trade inspector before being passed for passenger-carrying traffic and their high standard of inspection was most stringent. In hilly districts, for instance, in addition to the normal hand-brake (at the driver's right hand) and the rheostatic electric braking (operated by the driver's left hand from the controller), the Board of Trade insisted on 'slipper-brakes' being provided. These comprised a 'slipper' track brake operated on the track by the revolving wheel at the driver's right hand, mounted on a sleeve which passed over the wheel brake spindle outside the hand-brake column. When descending steep hills, the slipper-brake was applied with a pressure suitable to the gradient and the car could then easily be controlled by the hand-brake. In addition, rail-sanding equipment was provided for operation by the driver on wet or greasy rails. The danger of a car running away was practically eliminated. The illustration opposite is of the Penge route, Croydon, undergoing a Board of Trade inspection after construction; the Bristol tramcar above also illustrates the same type of slipper-brake on both tramcars.

What Might Have Been

Viewed in retrospect with detachment, and in comparison with the more enlightened cities and towns of the continent which retained and modernised their tramway systems and are now reaping the benefit of their foresight, the 'scrap the trams' campaign which gripped local authorities in Great Britain in the late 1940s seems even more amazing now than it did at the time. With our towns choking themselves to death with traffic congestion it is difficult to understand the belief that abandonment of tramways would provide even a temporary palliative. Towns which scrapped their tramcars soon discovered that fares rocketed. A factor which was not foreseen was the public resistance to buses, mainly due to their inefficient handling of large traffic flows, resulting in a marked drift from public to private transport. Again, in retrospect, it is astounding that Great Britain gave so little thought to the alternative of modernising and segregating the tramways, to provide a light rapid-transport system. Below is an example of 'what might have been' in Great Britain: the author standing by a modern streamlined rapid-transit tramcar at Scheveningen terminus in Holland. One of the Hague City Tramways fleet of silent high-capacity vehicles which run mainly on 'reserved' sleeper-track, providing a fast and efficient service.

One of the few British attempts to give a fair trial to a private right of way tramway track. This service ran from Leeds to Middleton, forsaking the streets at Moor Lane, a short distance from the city centre and taking a very picturesque course on sleeper-tracks through Middleton Woods. The picture shows a 'Middleton' bogie tramcar on a test run on this route.

The above picture of the upper saloon of LCC tramcar No 1 built in 1932 shows the high standard of luxury attained, the larger capacity of tramcars and the ample leg-room available.

An excellent example of a British light rapid-transit tramway reservation at Durham Road, Sunderland (*above*). The segregated sleeper-tracked tramway is entirely on the median-strip dividing the dual carriageways. Sunderland's tramcars were equipped with pantographs for current collection. Many German and other continental cities have adopted this principle and improved on the former British lead in this field by constructing tramway subways nearer the city centres thus making a 'tramway-metro' (considered to be as useful as a full-sized metropolitan railway) at much less cost.

Below is a streamlined Liverpool bogie tramcar speeding on sleeper-track along the median strip on the former splendid tramway system of that city.

Where the Trams Still Run

There are still three places in Great Britain where electric tramcars are successfully operated, two on public service and one at a very thriving and attractive museum. Pride of place for successful modern streamlined electric tramcars moving vast crowds goes to up-to-date and far-sighted Blackpool. The illustration below of Blackpool's modern depot shows three types of their fleet, single-deckers, a double-decker (seating ninety-four passengers) and an open 'toast-rack'.

The only other remaining electric tramway operating a well-used public service is the 3ft gauge Isle of Man 'Manx Electric Railway' running between Douglas and Ramsey on private right-of-way sleeper-track. Both Blackpool and the Manx Electric Railway provide panoramic views of long stretches of sea and are popular with holidaymakers.

The Manx Electric Railway follows the American inter-urban type of tramway both in its segregated track and rolling stock, although British built. The illustration above is of a bogie-car towing an open bogie-trailer at Derby Castle, Douglas in 1894, while below is seen an open toast-rack bogie-car towing a similar type of trailer at the same spot in 1968. The Manx Electric Railway also operates the Snaefell Mountain Railway, a 3ft 6in gauge electric line connecting with the MER at Laxey and climbing to Snaefell summit (2,034ft) in over $4\frac{1}{2}$ miles by adhesion only, without the aid of rack and pinion.

The mecca of all electric tramway enthusiasts in Great Britain is Crich, near Matlock in Derbyshire. In 1948, prompted by the realisation that tramcars were disappearing from our streets without trace and no established body seemed prepared to preserve suitable specimens, a small band of enthusiasts commenced the immense task themselves, finally in 1955 forming the Tramway Museum Society. Members gave their services, acquired the site of a former mineral railway built by the renowned George Stephenson, developed it against overwhelming odds and, over the years, have acquired over forty tramcars representative of England, Scotland, Ireland, Wales and a few from overseas countries. Tremendous efforts resulted in laying sufficient trackwork, erecting poles and overhead wires and in 1964, after the installation of a power supply and inspection to the standard of the Ministry of Transport, opening the line for passenger transport. The society is entirely dependent on voluntary contributions and, being centrally situated in England, carries over 120,000 passengers a year, crowds journeying thence from a wide area. The illustration above is of the depots with a former Glasgow tramcar in the foreground on its way towards the new extension track. This tramway is frequently in demand by film and television producers requiring contemporary sequences of former British street scenes in which the 'atmosphere' of electric tramcars is essential.

A modern Blackpool railcoach speeding along its private right-of-way, unimpeded by other traffic, operating to an efficient schedule, an excellent example of urban passenger transport.

British Electric Tramways Undertakings

MUNICIPALLY OWNED

Town	Gauge ft	in	Opening-Closing Dates
Aberdare	3	6	1913-1935
Aberdeen	4	8½	1899-1958
Accrington	4	0	1907-1932
Ashton-under-Lyne	4	8½	1902-1938
Ayr	4	8½	1901-1931
Barking	4	8½	1903-1929
Barrow	4	0	1904-1932
Batley	4	8½	1903-1932
Belfast	4	8½	1905-1954
Bexley	4	8½	1903-1935
Birkenhead	4	8½	1901-1937
Birmingham	3	6	1904-1953
Blackburn	4	0	1899-1949
Blackpool (including Fleetwood)	4	8½	1885-still operating
Bolton	4	8½	1900-1947
Bournemouth	3	6	1902-1936
Bradford	4	0	1898-1950
Brighton	3	6	1901-1939
Burnley	4	0	1901-1935
Burton-on-Trent	3	6	1903-1929
Bury	4	8½	1903-1949
Cardiff	4	8½	1902-1950
Chester	3	6	1903-1930
Chesterfield	4	8½	1904-1927
Colchester	3	6	1904-1929
Colne	4	0	1903-1934
Coventry	3	6	1895-1940
Croydon	4	8½	1901-1951
Darlington	3	6	1904-1926
Dartford	4	8½	1906-1935
Darwen	4	0	1900-1946
Derby	4	0	1904-1934
Doncaster	4	8½	1902-1935
Dover	3	6	1897-1936
Dundee	4	8½	1900-1956
East Ham	4	8½	1901-1940
Edinburgh	4	8½	1922-1956
Erith	4	8½	1905-1935
Exeter	3	6	1905-1931
Glasgow	4	7¾	1898-1962
Gloucester	3	6	1904-1933
Grimsby	4	8½	1901-1937
Halifax	3	6	1898-1939
Huddersfield	4	7¾	1901-1940
Hull	4	8½	1899-1945
Ilford	4	8½	1903-1938
Ilkeston	3	6	1903-1931
Ipswich	3	6	1903-1926
Keighley	4	0	1904-1924
Kilmarnock	4	8½	1904-1926
Kirkcaldy	3	6	1903-1931
Lancaster	4	8½	1903-1930
Leeds	4	8½	1897-1959
Leicester	4	8½	1904-1949
Leith	4	8½	1905-1920★
Leyton	4	8½	1906-1939
Lincoln	4	8½	1905-1929
Liverpool	4	8½	1898-1957
London	4	8½	1903-1952
Lowestoft	3	6	1903-1931
Luton	4	8½	1908-1932
Lytham St Annes	4	8½	1903-1937
Maidstone	3	6	1904-1930
Manchester	4	8½	1901-1949
Middlesbrough	3	6	1898-1934
Nelson	4	0	1903-1934
Newcastle-on-Tyne	4	8½	1901-1950
Newport	4	8½	1903-1937
Northampton	3	6	1904-1934
Nottingham	4	8½	1901-1936
Oldham	4	8½	1900-1946
Perth	3	6	1905-1929
Plymouth	3	6	1899-1945
Pontypridd	3	6	1905-1931
Portsmouth	4	7¾	1901-1936
Preston	4	8½	1904-1935
Rawtenstall	4	0	1909-1932
Reading	4	0	1903-1939
Rochdale	4	8½	1902-1932
Rotherham	4	8½	1903-1949
Salford	4	8½	1901-1947
Sheffield	4	8½	1899-1960
St Helens	4	8½	1900-1936
Southampton	4	8½	1900-1949
Southend	3	6	1901-1942
Southport	4	8½	1900-1934
South Shields	4	8½	1906-1946
Stockport	4	8½	1901-1951
Stockton	3	6	1898-1931
Sunderland	4	8½	1900-1954
Swindon	3	6	1904-1929
Wallasey	4	8½	1902-1933
Walsall	3	6	1902-1933
Walthamstow	4	8½	1905-1939
Warrington	4	8½	1902-1935
West Ham	4	8½	1904-1940
West Hartlepool	3	6	1896-1927
Wigan	{3	6	1901-1931
	{4	8½	
Wolverhampton	3	6	1902-1928
Yarmouth	3	6	1902-1933
York	3	6	1910-1935

★ Taken over by Edinburgh at this date

Town	Gauge ft	in	Opening-Closing Dates	Town	Gauge ft	in	Opening-Closing Dates
Aberdeen Suburban	4	8½	1904-1927	Llanelly & District	4	8½	1911-1933
Airdrie & Coatbridge	4	7¾	1904-1956	London United Tramways	4	8½	1901-1936
Barnsley	4	8½	1902-1930	Mansfield District	4	8½	1905-1932
Bath	4	8½	1904-1939	Manx Electric	3	0	1893-still operating
Bessbrook & Newry	3	0	1885-1948				
Birmingham & Midland	3	6	1904-1930	Merthyr	3	6	1901-1939
Bristol	4	8½	1895-1941	Metropolitan Electric	4	8½	1904-1939
Burton & Ashby	3	6	1906-1927	Mexborough & Swinton	4	8½	1907-1929
Camborne & Redruth	3	6	1902-1927	Middleton (Lancs)	4	8½	1902-1935
Carlisle	3	6	1900-1931	Musselburgh & District	4	8½	1904-1954
Chatham & District	3	6	1902-1930	Norwich	3	6	1900-1935
Cheltenham & District	3	6	1901-1930	Notts & Derbyshire	4	8½	1913-1932
Cork Electric Tramway	2	11½	1898-1931	Paisley & District	4	7¾	1904-1957
Cruden Bay	3	6	1899-1932	Peterborough	3	6	1903-1930
Dearne District	4	8½	1924-1933	Portsdown & Horndean	4	7¾	1903-1935
Dewsbury & Ossett	4	8½	1908-1933	Potteries	4	0	1899-1928
Douglas Southern Electric	4	8½	1896-1939	Rhondda	3	6	1908-1934
Dublin United Tramway Co	5	3	1896-1949	Rothesay	3	6	1902-1936
Dudley & Stourbridge	3	6	1899-1930	Scarborough	3	6	1904-1931
Dumbarton	4	7¾	1907-1928	Sheerness	3	6	1903-1917
Dundee, Broughty Ferry	4	8½	1905-1931	Snaefell Mountain	3	6	1895-still operating
Dunfermline	3	6	1909-1937				
Falkirk	4	0	1905-1936	South Lancs Tramway Co	4	8½	1903-1933
Gateshead	4	8½	1901-1951	South Metropolitan	4	8½	1906-1937
Giant's Causeway	3	0	1883-1949	South Staffordshire	3	6	1893-1930
Glossop	4	8½	1903-1927	Stalybridge	4	8½	1904-1945
Gosport & Fareham	4	7¾	1906-1929	Sunderland District	4	8½	1905-1925
Gravesend & Northfleet	4	8½	1901-1929	Swansea	4	8½	1900-1937
Great Crosby	4	8½	1900-1925	Swansea & Mumbles	4	8½	1929-1960
Great Grimsby	4	8½	1901-1937	Taunton	3	6	1901-1921
Greenock & Port Glasgow	4	7¾	1901-1929	Torquay	3	6	1907-1934
Grimsby & Immingham	4	8½	1912-1961	Tynemouth	3	6	1901-1931
Guernsey	4	8½	1892-1934	Tyneside	4	8½	1902-1930
Hastings	3	6	1905-1929	Wemyss & District	3	6	1906-1932
Hill of Howth	5	3	1901-1959	Weston-super-Mare	4	8½	1902-1937
Isle of Thanet	3	6	1901-1937	Wolverhampton District	3	6	1900-1928
Jarrow	4	8½	1906-1929	Worcester	3	6	1904-1928
Kidderminster & Stourport	3	6	1898-1929	Wrexham & District	3	6	1903-1927
Lanarkshire Tr Co	4	7¾	1903-1931	Yorkshire (West Riding)	4	8½	1904-1932
Leamington & Warwick	3	6	1905-1930	Yorkshire Woollen District	4	8½	1903-1934
Llandudno & Colwyn Bay	3	6	1907-1956				

In a few systems with a departure from the more usual 3ft 6in, 4ft and 4ft 8½in gauges, it will be noticed that the peculiar gauge of 4ft 7¾in was adopted (notably in the Clyde Valley area). This was to enable railway wagons to be run on the tramway tracks. The depth of the flange of a railway wagon is greater than the depth of the groove of a tram rail and so the railway wagons had to run on the flanges of their wheels instead of on their tyres, the taper of the flanges necessitating a reduction of tramway gauge of ¾in. Some commercial firms in Glasgow owned their own electric locomotives for hauling railway wagons loaded with coal and other materials between their works and railway sidings over the tramway tracks by arrangement with the tramway undertaking.

The foregoing table of British electric tramway undertakings gives the names of the towns initially operating electric tramways or the dates they electrified their previous horse or steam tramways. In some cases the identity of the original operators had been changed by its being merged or absorbed; in these cases the closure date indicates the demise of the original electric tramway undertakings.

In Ashton-under-Lyne, Barrow in Furness, Birmingham, Colne, Coventry, Devonport, Grimsby, Lytham St Annes, Middlesbrough, Poole, Shipley, Southport, Stockton, St Helens, Walsall and West Hartlepool electric tramcars were introduced and operated by companies before being taken over by the municipal authorities; also in some cases municipalities owned the lines in their areas allowing them to be operated by companies.

Sources of Illustrations and Acknowledgements

W. E. Robertson, coloured frontispiece and jacket
The Press Association Ltd, models picture on back of jacket
Edgar Allen Engineering Ltd, 1, 11
Glasgow Corporation Transport Department, 2, 24, 25 (top), 27, 36, 46, 52, 53, 55, 84, 86, 90
London Transport Executive, 6, 12, 16, 43, 47, 48, 56, 57, 58, 59, 60, 79, 80, 87, 89
Greater London Council, 10, 34 (top), 62, 82, 96
Tramway Museum Society, 13, 64 (top), 106
Brush Electrical Engineering Co Ltd, 14
Author's collection, 15, 18, 19 (top), 31 (bottom), 67 (top), 100, 104
J. H. Price, 17 (top and bottom), 35, 63 (bottom), 72, 102
The John Appleby Collection, 19 (bottom), 25 (bottom), 39 (middle)
Bristol Omnibus Co Ltd, 20 (top), 34 (bottom), 40 (bottom), 70, 99
Hurst Nelson & Co Ltd, 20 (bottom), 23, 42 (top)
Cassiers Magazine, 21 (top)
W. A. Camwell, 21 (bottom), 76
R. B. Parr, 22, 61 (bottom), 63 (top), 66 (bottom), 68, 93
Maley & Taunton Ltd, 26, 42 (bottom), 45 (bottom), 97, 101
Photochrom Co, 28 and back of jacket
R. Elliott, 29 (top)
The late F. J. Roche, 29 (bottom), 32 (top), 35 (bottom), 38
W. J. Haynes, 30 (top and bottom), 31, 33 (top), 37 (bottom), 39 (bottom), 69 (bottom), 85, 107
The Light Railway Transport League, 33 (bottom)
Robert H. Mack, 37 (top)
J. H. Meredith, 39 (top)
Mather & Platt Ltd, 40 (top), 105 (top)
Express and Star, Wolverhampton, 41
English Electric-AEI Traction Ltd, 44, 45 (top)
J. S. Webb, 49 (top and bottom), 78
West Midlands Passenger Transport Executive, 50, 61 (top)
Fox Photos Ltd, 51
W. J. Wyse, 55
D. Conrad, 64 (bottom)
A. D. Packer, 65
Tramway & Light Railway Society, 66 (top), 73
County Borough of Huddersfield Passenger Transport Department, 67 (bottom)
Aberdeen Corporation Transport Department, 69 (top)
Colchester Borough Transport, 71 (top)
Ian M. Coonie, 71 (bottom)
H. E. Jordan, 74, 75
The South Wales Transport Company Ltd, 77
H. B. Priestley, 81, 94
Western Daily Express, 83
Bernard Lane, 88
M. J. O'Connor, 91

Merseyside Passenger Transport Executive, 92
West Lancashire Evening Gazette, 95
The Glasgow Herald, 98 (top)
Lens, 98 (bottom)
Alan A. Jackson, 103 (top)
R. J. Wiseman, 103 (bottom)
D. J. Mitchell, 105 (bottom)

The author is most grateful for all the help and ready co-operation he has received from the photographers and others listed above. He would also like to thank the following for their interest and assistance: Mr H. Stead, Manager, Trackwork Division, Edgar Allen Engineering Ltd; Mr W. Murray, MInstT, General Manager, Glasgow Corporation Transport; Miss E. D. Mercer, BA, FSA, Head Archivist, and Miss R. Watson, Photograph Librarian, both of Greater London Record Office and Library; the staff of London Transport Executive Photographic Library; Mr J. H. Price; Mr H. G. Kelvin, Mather & Platt Ltd; Miss M. Oldbury; Mr G. B. Claydon, LLB; Mr A. W. Maley, Maley & Taunton Ltd; Mr N. Gardener, English Electric-AEI Traction Ltd; Miss Gillian Huddy.

Index